Gratitude Journal

name	
address	
email	
phone	
others	

MW00914688

Inspirational Quote

	Emergency Contact
name	
address	
email	
phone	
relationship	
others	

table of contents

A smooth sea never made a skilled sailor.

FRANKLIN D. ROOSEVELT

PLEASE LEAVE A REVIEW BECAUSE
WE WOULD LIKE TO HERE YOUR
FEEDBACK AND SUGGESTIONS TO
MAKE BETTER PRODUCTS
AND SERVICES FOR YOU.

**YOU ARE REALLY
APPRECIATED!**

hope you like it.

GET MORE BOOKS,
SCAN HERE!

page	description

Date:

Quote of the Day

Today I am truly grateful for

Here's what would make today great

I am thankful for...

Some amazing things that happened today

What could I have done to make today even better?

Gratitude Journal

Here's what would
make today great

Today I am truly
grateful for

Quote of the Day

What could I have
done to make today
even better?

Some amazing
things that
happened today

I am thankful for...

Date:

Here's what would
make today great

Quote of the Day

Today I am truly
grateful for

What could I have
done to make today
even better?

I am thankful for...

Some amazing
things that
happened today

Gratitude Journal

Date: _____

Today I am truly grateful for

Quote of the Day

Here's what would make today great

Some amazing things that happened today

I am thankful for...

What could I have done to make today even better?

Date:

Gratitude Journal

Here's what would make today great

Today I am truly grateful for

Quote of the Day

What could I have done to make today even better?

Some amazing things that happened today

I am thankful for...

Gratitude Journal

Date: _____

Quote of the Day

Today I am truly grateful for

Here's what would make today great

I am thankful for...

Some amazing things that happened today

What could I have done to make today even better?

Gratitude Journal

Quote of the Day

Today I am truly
grateful for

Here's what would
make today great

I am thankful for...

Some amazing
things that
happened today

What could I have
done to make today
even better?

Gratitude Journal

Here's what would make today great

Today I am truly grateful for

Quote of the Day

What could I have done to make today even better?

Some amazing things that happened today

I am thankful for...

Date:

Here's what would
make today great

Quote of the Day

Today I am truly
grateful for

What could I have
done to make today
even better?

I am thankful for...

Some amazing
things that
happened today

Gratitude Journal

Date:

Today I am truly grateful for

Quote of the Day

Here's what would make today great

Some amazing things that happened today

I am thankful for...

What could I have done to make today even better?

Date.

Here's what would
make today great

Today I am truly
grateful for

Quote of the Day

What could I have
done to make today
even better?

Some amazing
things that
happened today

I am thankful for...

Gratitude Journal

Date:

Quote of the Day

Today I am truly grateful for

Here's what would make today great

I am thankful for...

Some amazing things that happened today

What could I have done to make today even better?

Date:

Quote of the Day

Today I am truly
grateful for

Here's what would
make today great

I am thankful for...

Some amazing
things that
happened today

What could I have
done to make today
even better?

Gratitude Journal

Date:

Here's what would make today great

Today I am truly grateful for

Quote of the Day

What could I have done to make today even better?

Some amazing things that happened today

I am thankful for...

Date:

Quote of the Day

Here's what would make today great

Today I am truly grateful for

What could I have done to make today even better?

I am thankful for...

Some amazing things that happened today

Gratitude Journal

Today I am truly grateful for

Here's what would make today great

Quote of the Day

Some amazing things that happened today

I am thankful for...

What could I have done to make today even better?

Date:

Gratitude Journal

Here's what would make today great

Today I am truly grateful for

Quote of the Day

What could I have done to make today even better?

Some amazing things that happened today

I am thankful for...

Gratitude Journal

Date: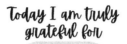

Quote of the Day

Today I am truly grateful for

Here's what would make today great

I am thankful for...

Some amazing things that happened today

What could I have done to make today even better?

Date: ████████████

Quote of the Day

Today I am truly grateful for

Here's what would make today great

I am thankful for...

Some amazing things that happened today

What could I have done to make today even better?

Gratitude Journal

Here's what would
make today great

Today I am truly
grateful for

Quote of the Day

What could I have
done to make today
even better?

Some amazing
things that
happened today

I am thankful for...

Date:

Here's what would
make today great

Quote of the Day

Today I am truly
grateful for

What could I have
done to make today
even better?

I am thankful for...

Some amazing
things that
happened today

Gratitude Journal

Today I am truly grateful for

Here's what would make today great

Quote of the Day

Some amazing things that happened today

What could I have done to make today even better?

I am thankful for...

Date,

Gratitude Journal

Here's what would make today great

Today I am truly grateful for

Quote of the Day

What could I have done to make today even better?

Some amazing things that happened today

I am thankful for...

Gratitude Journal

Quote of the Day

Today I am truly grateful for

Here's what would make today great

I am thankful for...

Some amazing things that happened today

What could I have done to make today even better?

Gratitude Journal

Quote of the Day

Today I am truly grateful for

Here's what would make today great

I am thankful for...

Some amazing things that happened today

What could I have done to make today even better?

Gratitude Journal

Here's what would
make today great

Today I am truly
grateful for

Quote of the Day

What could I have
done to make today
even better?

Some amazing
things that
happened today

I am thankful for...

Date:

Here's what would
make today great

Quote of the Day

Today I am truly
grateful for

What could I have
done to make today
even better?

I am thankful for...

Some amazing
things that
happened today

Gratitude Journal

Date:

Today I am truly grateful for

Here's what would make today great

Quote of the Day

Some amazing things that happened today

I am thankful for...

What could I have done to make today even better?

Gratitude Journal

Here's what would make today great

Today I am truly grateful for

Quote of the Day

What could I have done to make today even better?

Some amazing things that happened today

I am thankful for...

Gratitude Journal

Quote of the Day

Today I am truly grateful for

Here's what would make today great

I am thankful for...

Some amazing things that happened today

What could I have done to make today even better?

Date: _____

Gratitude Journal

Quote of the Day

Today I am truly grateful for

Here's what would make today great

I am thankful for...

Some amazing things that happened today

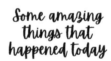

What could I have done to make today even better?

Gratitude Journal

Date:

Here's what would make today great

Today I am truly grateful for

Quote of the Day

What could I have done to make today even better?

Some amazing things that happened today

I am thankful for...

Date:

Gratitude Journal

Quote of the Day

Today I am truly grateful for

Here's what would make today great

I am thankful for...

Some amazing things that happened today

What could I have done to make today even better?

Gratitude Journal

Date:

Here's what would make today great

Today I am truly grateful for

Quote of the Day

What could I have done to make today even better?

Some amazing things that happened today

I am thankful for...

-35-

Date:

Here's what would
make today great

Quote of the Day

Today I am truly
grateful for

What could I have
done to make today
even better?

I am thankful for...

Some amazing
things that
happened today

Gratitude Journal

Today I am truly grateful for

Quote of the Day

Here's what would make today great

Some amazing things that happened today

What could I have done to make today even better?

I am thankful for...

Date: _____

Gratitude Journal

Here's what would make today great

Today I am truly grateful for

Quote of the Day

What could I have done to make today even better?

Some amazing things that happened today

I am thankful for...

Gratitude Journal

Date: _____

Quote of the Day

Today I am truly grateful for

Here's what would make today great

I am thankful for...

Some amazing things that happened today

What could I have done to make today even better?

Gratitude Journal

Quote of the Day

Today I am truly grateful for

Here's what would make today great

I am thankful for...

Some amazing things that happened today

What could I have done to make today even better?

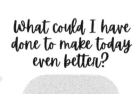

Gratitude Journal

Date:

Here's what would make today great

Today I am truly grateful for

Quote of the Day

What could I have done to make today even better?

Some amazing things that happened today

I am thankful for...

Date:

Here's what would
make today great

Quote of the Day

Today I am truly
grateful for

What could I have
done to make today
even better?

I am thankful for...

Some amazing
things that
happened today

Gratitude Journal

Date:

Today I am truly grateful for

Quote of the Day

Here's what would make today great

Some amazing things that happened today

I am thankful for...

What could I have done to make today even better?

Date:

Gratitude Journal

Here's what would make today great

Today I am truly grateful for

Quote of the Day

What could I have done to make today even better?

Some amazing things that happened today

I am thankful for...

Gratitude Journal

Date:

Quote of the Day

Today I am truly grateful for

Here's what would make today great

I am thankful for...

Some amazing things that happened today

What could I have done to make today even better?

Date: _____

Quote of the Day

Today I am truly
grateful for

Here's what would
make today great

I am thankful for...

Some amazing
things that
happened today

What could I have
done to make today
even better?

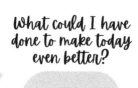

Gratitude Journal

Here's what would make today great

Today I am truly grateful for

Quote of the Day

What could I have done to make today even better?

Some amazing things that happened today

I am thankful for...

Date.

Here's what would
make today great

Quote of the Day

Today I am truly
grateful for

What could I have
done to make today
even better?

I am thankful for...

Some amazing
things that
happened today

Gratitude Journal

Date:

Today I am truly grateful for

Here's what would make today great

Quote of the Day

Some amazing things that happened today

What could I have done to make today even better?

I am thankful for...

Date:

Gratitude Journal

Here's what would make today great

Today I am truly grateful for

Quote of the Day

What could I have done to make today even better?

Some amazing things that happened today

I am thankful for...

Gratitude Journal

Date:

Quote of the Day

Today I am truly grateful for

Here's what would make today great

I am thankful for...

Some amazing things that happened today

What could I have done to make today even better?

Quote of the Day

Today I am truly grateful for

Here's what would make today great

I am thankful for...

Some amazing things that happened today

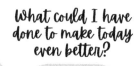

What could I have done to make today even better?

Gratitude Journal

Date: _____

Here's what would make today great

Today I am truly grateful for

Quote of the Day

What could I have done to make today even better?

Some amazing things that happened today

I am thankful for...

Date.

Quote of the Day

Here's what would make today great

Today I am truly grateful for

I am thankful for...

What could I have done to make today even better?

Some amazing things that happened today

Gratitude Journal

Date:

Today I am truly grateful for

Quote of the Day

Here's what would make today great

Some amazing things that happened today

I am thankful for...

What could I have done to make today even better?

Date: _____

Gratitude Journal

Here's what would
make today great

Today I am truly
grateful for

Quote of the Day

What could I have
done to make today
even better?

Some amazing
things that
happened today

I am thankful for...

Gratitude Journal

Quote of the Day

Today I am truly
grateful for

Here's what would
make today great

I am thankful for...

Some amazing
things that
happened today

What could I have
done to make today
even better?

Date. _____

Quote of the Day

Today I am truly
grateful for

Here's what would
make today great

I am thankful for...

Some amazing
things that
happened today

What could I have
done to make today
even better?

Gratitude Journal

Date:

Here's what would make today great

Today I am truly grateful for

Quote of the Day

What could I have done to make today even better?

Some amazing things that happened today

I am thankful for...

Date:

Here's what would make today great

Quote of the Day

Today I am truly grateful for

What could I have done to make today even better?

I am thankful for...

Some amazing things that happened today

Gratitude Journal

Today I am truly grateful for

Quote of the Day

Here's what would make today great

Some amazing things that happened today

I am thankful for...

What could I have done to make today even better?

Date:

Gratitude Journal

Here's what would make today great

Today I am truly grateful for

Quote of the Day

What could I have done to make today even better?

Some amazing things that happened today

I am thankful for...

Gratitude Journal

Date:

Quote of the Day

Today I am truly grateful for

Here's what would make today great

I am thankful for...

Some amazing things that happened today

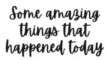

What could I have done to make today even better?

Gratitude Journal

Quote of the Day

Today I am truly grateful for

Here's what would make today great

I am thankful for...

Some amazing things that happened today

What could I have done to make today even better?

Gratitude Journal

Here's what would make today great

Today I am truly grateful for

Quote of the Day

What could I have done to make today even better?

Some amazing things that happened today

I am thankful for...

Date.

Here's what would
make today great

Quote of the Day

Today I am truly
grateful for

What could I have
done to make today
even better?

I am thankful for...

Some amazing
things that
happened today

Gratitude Journal

Today I am truly grateful for

Quote of the Day

Here's what would make today great

Some amazing things that happened today

I am thankful for...

What could I have done to make today even better?

Date:

Gratitude Journal

Here's what would make today great

Today I am truly grateful for

Quote of the Day

What could I have done to make today even better?

Some amazing things that happened today

I am thankful for...

Gratitude Journal

Date: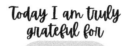

Quote of the Day

Today I am truly grateful for

Here's what would make today great

I am thankful for...

Some amazing things that happened today

What could I have done to make today even better?

Gratitude Journal

Quote of the Day

Today I am truly grateful for

Here's what would make today great

I am thankful for...

Some amazing things that happened today

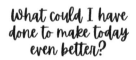

What could I have done to make today even better?

Gratitude Journal

Date:

Here's what would make today great

Today I am truly grateful for

Quote of the Day

What could I have done to make today even better?

Some amazing things that happened today

I am thankful for...

Date.

Gratitude Journal

Quote of the Day

Here's what would make today great

Today I am truly grateful for

I am thankful for...

What could I have done to make today even better?

Some amazing things that happened today

Gratitude Journal

Date:

Today I am truly grateful for

Quote of the Day

Here's what would make today great

Some amazing things that happened today

I am thankful for...

What could I have done to make today even better?

Date:

Gratitude Journal

Here's what would
make today great

Today I am truly
grateful for

Quote of the Day

What could I have
done to make today
even better?

Some amazing
things that
happened today

I am thankful for...

Gratitude Journal

Quote of the Day

Today I am truly grateful for

Here's what would make today great

I am thankful for...

Some amazing things that happened today

What could I have done to make today even better?

Gratitude Journal

Quote of the Day

Today I am truly grateful for

Here's what would make today great

I am thankful for...

Some amazing things that happened today

What could I have done to make today even better?

Gratitude Journal

Here's what would make today great

Today I am truly grateful for

Quote of the Day

What could I have done to make today even better?

Some amazing things that happened today

I am thankful for...

Date:

Here's what would
make today great

Quote of the Day

Today I am truly
grateful for

What could I have
done to make today
even better?

I am thankful for...

Some amazing
things that
happened today

Gratitude Journal

Date:

Today I am truly grateful for

Quote of the Day

Here's what would make today great

Some amazing things that happened today

I am thankful for...

What could I have done to make today even better?

Date:

Gratitude Journal

Here's what would make today great

Today I am truly grateful for

Quote of the Day

What could I have done to make today even better?

Some amazing things that happened today

I am thankful for...

Gratitude Journal

Date:

Quote of the Day

Today I am truly grateful for

Here's what would make today great

I am thankful for...

Some amazing things that happened today

What could I have done to make today even better?

Sketch and Note:

Date:

Sketch and Note:

Sketch and Note:

Date:

Sketch and Note:

Sketch and Note:

Date:

Sketch and Note:

Sketch and Note:

Sketch and Note:

Date:

Sketch and Note:

Date:

Sketch and Note:

Sketch and Note:

Date:

Sketch and Note:

Date:

Date:

Sketch and Note:

Made in the USA
Monee, IL
11 October 2021